Sagittariusly

BLUNT!

Danielle Dixon

Sagittariusly **BLUNT!**© 2017 by *Danielle Dixon*

.

For information contact: info@uptownmediaventures.com

Book and Cover design by Team Uptown

ISBN: 978-1-68121-086-5

First Edition: November 2017

Sankofa
Freedom Press

10 9 8 7 6 5 4 3 2 1

Dedicated to all of the voiceless people who never thought anyone would want to hear their story. Keep working, keep writing, keep expressing your truth. When you share your story, you heal yourself and the world!

Table of Contents

Danielle Dixon

Ain't Dat Some Shit?

What If...
>Your parents didn't fail you?

What if...
>Their assignment with you
>Was to keep you alive until you could keep
yourself?
>And look at you now
>Livin' and shit!

>Ain't dat some shit?
>Ain't DAT some shit?

What if...
>They were just mere mortals with issues?

What if...
>They learned more from you
>Than you ever could from them?

What if...
>Your strength
>Turns out to be their salvation?

>Ain't dat some shit?
>Ain't DAT some shit?

What if...
>That narrative you tell the world
>'bout how "It's just Me, Myself, and I"
>That you say is your mantra
>Because it steel's your nerves

So you don't get disappointed by a world that
doesn't love you
Actually, creates the reality
That the world doesn't love you?
What if...
Love never came to stay
Because You
Never set a place for it at your table?
But you shacked up
With that crush   you swore you couldn't
breathe without
Whose presence choked the life out of you.

Ain't dat some shit?
Ain't DAT some shit?
What if...
You had help the whole time
But never asked for it?
What if...
The guardian angel
That wants so badly to help you succeed
Sits bound, gagged and forgotten
By YOUR negativity and lack of action?

Ain't dat some
shit?
Ain't DAT some shit?
What if...
Our reality
Is someone else's short sighted version
Of a fantasy?

And...
What if...
The unrealistic things we fantasize about
Are the things we really are capable of?
What if...
Normalcy
Was really abnormal
And dysfunction
Is the first sign you're alive?
What if...
Conformity creates chaos?
What if...
You never struggled?
What if...
You never felt the urgency
Of needing to achieve your goal the first time
Because there's an ass whoopin'
Waiting for your failure?
What if...
You never learned the lessons
You got from the struggle
That forged you into the warrior you are today?
What if...
The lesson is in the process
And not the result?

Ain't dat some shit?
Ain't DAT some shit?

Danielle N Dixon
10/28/2016

Danielle Dixon

Beautiful Jellyfish

Your soul glowed luminescent
I was drawn to your light
You floated through life
Graceful and lithe
I loved your transparence
No games
No hidden agendas
I bought into an idea of "us"
Problem was
I could see right through you
No spine
No substance
You were just a beautiful jellyfish
Who stood for nothing
And was poisonous to the touch

Danielle N Dixon 5/2016

Danielle Dixon

12

Beware

Beware of the slave

That don't wanna be free

They'll sell you out

If you try to flee

Their only goal for crowning grace

Is just to take the master's place.

Danielle N Dixon
7-15-2016

Black Guilt

I found my long lost brother today
He was waiting for a bus in the rain
He had a look of defeat and disdain
And I didn't want to claim him

So, I covered my face
And tried to push by
But we locked eyes
And I couldn't deny him.

Dirt under his finger nails
Mud on his shoes
Hair unkempt
Sweatin' 80 proof

Asked for a cigarette
Then he asked for a ride
Could I spare a coupla dollars
For a brotha's hard time?

He was running his same ol shit
But I dared not say no
I was already convicted of the crime of
"actin' funny"
In the black court of law.

"It sho' is a blessin' to see you
Out here in this weather
You know us black folks
Gots ta stick tuhgetha"

That's the line he used
To get me to see things his way
But a simple ride around the corner with him
Could commandeer my whole day

A ride to the whiskey store,
the numbers house and something to eat
I wondered if the stench of poverty
Would ever wash clean off my leather seats

So, I apologized
Shrugged my shoulders
Can't help you out today
But my black guilt gave him $50
To make him go away

Danielle N Dixon
11/5/2017

Freak Flag

I wanna know how high
Does your freak flag fly

Blowing in the wind
For all the world to see
Or does your flag
          only rise up the pole for me
'Cause I'm a
          snake charmer
Blowing on that flute
Slide on up that pole
And salute

If I rub your magic lamp
Will a genie pop out?
Grant my love desires
And make me wild out?
Give me the vapors
Open up my nose
Rip off my panty hose
Turn this poetry to prose?

Makes me wonder 'bout how you learned that
And I don't give a damn where your girl at
Ain't even gotta ask can we do that
My Freak flags' flyin' high
 But you knew that

Cause you don't love 'em
You hit 'em
Got much swag in your denim
Let me swab your mouth
If you ain't spittin' no venom

Before I let you know
How deep this rabbit hole goes...
I need to find out
 if you're fit for the cause

You may just be the man
Who can ring my bell
   But
Are there any serpents in your wishing well?

If your results don't fail
We gone show and don't tell
My freak flag just fell
My fantasy just got real
Pregnancies. Diseases
Uh!
Moment killers
When I'm tryna catch that moment when we're
Fuckin' like gorillas!

Danielle Dixon
7/9/2016

I Am Fabulous

I. Am. Fabulous!

I was fabulous 20 years ago
I'll be fabulous 20 years from now
When I'm dead
        I'll be dead and fabulous
I'll be fabulous at 500lbs or 99lbs soaking wet
I'm fabulous when I'm pretty
Being ugly doesn't stop me from being fabulous
I am fabulous in abundance
When I lack resources
        I'm resourcefully fabulous
I was born fabulous
        With the ability to generate fabulousness
My fabulous is a self- contained unit
It morphs, changes, and reinvents itself
        As it sees fit
My fabulous does not need your approval
Yet it remains open to be inspired
        By other people's fabulousness
Because the world needs fabulous people
Playing meek never inspired anyone
And when I see how you wear fabulousness
        Whether you strut it
        Sashay it
        Limp it
        Crutch it
        Or roll it in a wheelchair

Danielle Dixon

I will always applaud it
Because one person's fabulousness does not diminish another's
Fabulousness is infinite
And the world needs your rendition
> Of unapologetic fabulousness
> To be represented
> Right Here
> Right now
> Right where you stand

Danielle Dixon 8/5/2016

If I Fall Into Your Eyes

What adventure may I find
If I fall into your eyes?

Will I find that wondrous place where your dreams roam
free?
Where your wildest possibilities mature into realities?

Might I walk your epic battlefield
Where insurgent doubts get killed?
And break those chains of iniquity to set those captives
free?

What adventure may I find
If I fall into your eyes?

Will you allow me into your quiet place
Where you disrobe worry and haste
Lay down burdens of this world's course
And connect back with your higher source?

Might I fall into your flow
Where we slow grind low
And the clock winds slow
And intimacy grows?

Or will I plummet into your asylum

Where the darker you resides
And carnal natures rise
And we succumb to the tides?

What adventures will I find
If I fall into your eyes

Are there strong arms to catch me before I hit the
bottom?
Or shall I fall into a labyrinth
 Of mazes and tunnels?

Will I find our paths entwine and harmoniously become
one
Or is there a dead end with a broken bridge
Where I'll sink or swim alone
Can I navigate the flow of your ever -changing   tide?
If I die in your dreams
Will I die in real life?

What adventure will I find
If I fall into your eyes?

Danielle Dixon
4/9/2016

Long Lost Brethren

My soul hung in effigy
On a wall painted white
The holes have been filled
To mask the evidence
Of souls who hung here before
Awaiting the same fate

95 of 100 people passed me by
No second looks
No consideration
Not even a fuck you

95 people passed by the passion
Passed by the pride
Of rendering something to perfection
Passed by the angst of tearing down
That perfection
Because it's too perfect
to exist in a cohesive piece of work

Passed by the building up
Of the background
The supporting cast
Trying to make it as perfect as
Perfection once was
Worrying that perfection will never happen again twice
Fearing that I'm not good enough to pull it off

95 people passed by the 20+ times
I thought about giving up
And starting over

Passed by the 20+ times
I stepped outside of myself
Stood back from myself
Viewed myself from different distances
To see if my soul resonates the same
From across the room as it does up close

95 people rejected me
With an energy worse than hatred,
INDIFFERENCE

But
There were 5 people who stayed
5 people who noticed
5 people who read my hidden messages
5 people who recognized my Melody
 And sang the words with me

5 people saw my soul
Warmed themselves by it's fire
And will carry it's flame with them in spirit.

95 people passed me by
But the 5 who stayed
Are my long lost brethren
And those 5

Will return to the foreign lands
Where they have made their lives
They will tell our stories
And their souls may hang in effigy
In foreign arenas
And 95 people
Will pass them by
And they will wonder if they will die of such apathy
But the 5 who stay...
The members of our lost tribe
Will restore their faith in humanity
Will engage in conversations without words
Will commune
And commiserate
And instead of bombs bursting in air They'll be little heart emojis
And for that moment in time
They'll feel at home in a foreign land

They will no longer tell a story
About the 95 people who passed them by
But the 5 who stayed

Danielle N. Dixon
5/18/2017

Danielle Dixon

Magic Beans

So I sold this poor guy
Some magic beans
But what he bought
Were hopes and dreams
That returned a smile
To his serious face
Of what he would do with
      Just one golden egg

Sold a lady this painting
Of a loving couple hugged up close
But what she really bought
Was what she needed most

I sang this song
Of compassion and forgiveness
And he loves to hear me sing it
Each note is a prayer from his ears to God
That she will accept his repentance

Sold a lady a mirror
That said love starts here
Each glance sets in motion
Empowerment
      And love of self
That she couldn't get
From anywhere else

A religious man
  With no money to offer
  Puts 10% in the coffers
But what he really buys on Sundays
  Is nourishment to get through
  The other days
That may sound like a large sacrifice
But he ain't worried 'bout the price

Some say I'm a crook
      For selling intangible things
It's irresponsible for a poor guy
      To spend money on magic beans
But I say to the critics
It's no different
  Than you playing lottery
Mega Millions, Powerball, Pick three
And the hopes that rise

When the jackpot gets high
As you fantasize
Creative ways
  To kiss your job goodbye

See, there's nothing wrong with magic beans
When a dollar buys a dream
When we dream we lift our eyes
Concentrate on a bigger prize
This sets the universe in motion
To grant those things on which we focus

If we focus on our broke-ness
Our pockets will never be fixed
But if we focus on possibilities
Those ideas just may grow wings

The poor man planted his magic beans
Along with them his hopes and dreams
Watered and nurtured them all through spring
Believing he'd yield delightful things

As the first buds broke through the top soil
So budded other endeavors
 He'd been working on
As he harvested a plentiful crop
Plentiful energies blessed his house

While he never saw a beanstalk, golden egg or   goose
He did learn to plant dream seeds
And harvest all their fruit

I sold this poem
To a hopeful group
And they gladly paid me forward
Because it spoke their truth

Danielle N Dixon
5/2016

Midnight Caller

My pocket buzzed

I knew what it was

My mid-night call to love

He's not the man I want

But he satisfies *THIS* need

So we creep

Discreet

But

Sometimes

When he holds my hand

Talks about his kids

His fam

I see

A man...

And not just a dick in a glass case

My desire deflates

Feeling suddenly

Puritanically chaste

I leave

Post haste.

Danielle N Dixon 2013

My Love Song

My love song ain't dainty
My love song ain't cute
My love song ain't pretty
Cause it's all about that nitty gritty

I don't need your money
You don't need no pickup line
I've already sized you up
So let's stop wastin' time

I ain't got no children
I ain't got no man
I ain't got no worries see
I do just what I damned well please

I party when I want to
I can stay out all night
I ain't gotta check in
And I ain't gotta lie

I ain't no domestic goddess
I wear sweat pants to bed
If you're fine with it I cool with that
If not then I'm still cool with that

I may not put on make up
I may not paint my nails
My love song ain't pretty

It's just all about that nitty gritty

If you're not too sensitive
  And like to keep it real
Then wear that prophylactic baby
  We can make a deal

No I do not loan out money
I ain't callin' you my man
I ain't tryna meet your mama
Catching feelings would be bad

I ain't gon' be your ride or die
I damned sho ain't your bitch
You're my flavor for tonight
  But tomorrow I might switch

Love me then leave me
I'm tellin' you it's cool
'Cause if you ever stuck around
  You'd be in my way fool

My life is built to suit me
Now, you messin' with my flow
If you can't hang with my speed of life
Then you gon' hafta go

I ain't one of those "New Age" chicks
Sayin' they don't need no man
But truly there's a lot of shit

I've done all by myself

My love song ain't bitter
My love song ain't sweet
My love song ain't witty
But it's all about that nitty gritty

Don't want to diminish
Your value as a man
But if your value's based on what I need
Then sexual healing's what I need

So get in where you fit in
And don't study me too long
If you think about it too hard baby
You gon' learn me wrong

If you're searching for companionship
To keep your life on track
I suggest you run go find her
I ain't tryna hold you back

I will never sweat you for your love
That's just not how I roll
If you need to leave I'm cool with that
If not then I'm still cool with that

My love song ain't cozy
My love does not fall
My love song ain't no love song
      At all.

Danielle Dixon
Started 2013
Revised and finished
7/2016

My Muthaf**ka

Solitude is my *muthafucka*
I could love no other
My lover is an empath's dream
We make love to silence
        And have threesomes with emotionally safe
places
Our love rejuvenates
        Replenishes spent energies

This glow on my face
Is what our love made
Makes outsiders cup their eyes
Scheming 'bout how to muscle in on my shine
But those bleeding hearts can't handle my wine
Shiiiid...I'm 120 proof all the time
They want that "ready-made" love
They didn't work to find

The instant gratification
Of sexual validation
I just can't provide
'Cause there's no combination
Of loveless relations
To fix their wounded pride

So I juke left
And I slide right
To let them pass me by

Hoping that they miss me with that
NONSTOP CHAOTIC CHATTER!
From the souls of their conquests
Won in battle
Telling their unrequited love stories
And devil's illusions
Don't need clairaudience to hear the confusion
Trying to get between me and my lover
My muthafucka
Love they can never have
Because their noise rapes silence
And they'll never have emotionally safe spaces
When they collect souls like badges of honor

Contd…

Why would I cheat my lover?
With these lecherous
  Homeless ass
    "It's Cuffin' season"
      Suckas!

Solitude is MY Muthafucka!
And I could love no other!

Danielle N Dixon
12/14/2016

My Own Superhero

Because Prince Charming was too late
    My Innocence was lost and I was already awake
Because my chariot turns into a pumpkin at midnight
    And it's too easy to lose glass slippers when
you're trying to beat the clock
    So I lace mine up now because I'm gon' to hafta
walk
Because knights in shining armor need damsels in
distress to justify their existence
    And my knight needed more help than me
    So I bandaged up his cracked, bloodied armor and
set him free
Because I'm seen as a lioness who can hunt her own
prey
    So no one asked me if I ate today
Because Home is a war zone
    But it's the war I know
    So I'll click my sneakers three times to get back
there
Because Paradise ain't takin' no refugees
Because War said "The World Is A Ghetto"
    And they were right
Because we see the green grass on the other side
    But not the shit that fertilized it
Because there is nowhere else to go that doesn't require
struggle
Because there is no glory without the battle
Because the babies won't have a choice

But to make a difference
In this world that we're trying to get away from
Because I saw a rose grow up through the cracks in the concrete
Because Hope is all I've got and my optimism is keeping me up
Because for every NO, every turn down, every shut out I get
I see four more ways that *I* can do it better
Because without vision the people perish
Because I've piggy backed off the shoulders of my ancestors
And I owe them this much
Because I'm tired but not defeated
So I search to find my crack in the concrete
Because I'm that weed fear couldn't kill
Because my super cape is tested but not torn
Because I have a chance today to do it better than yesterday
Because a sliver of daylight shined on *me* through that break in the clouds

So, I'll be my own Super hero
Because I'm the one who can
Because I'm made for this.

My Nigga

See…
I'm real sick
Trying to ween myself
Off the word
Nigga
My one word everything
My friend…My nigga
My lover…My nigga
My enemy…That nigga
The idiot…This nigga
The catch 'em in a lie phrase…Nigga Please!
Our one word checkmate
To subjugate our humanity
A one word reminder
You can't be who you want to be
But, it's time to get clean
Define who I was meant to be
Words are things that define our being
Living out the slave master's creed
Ain't working for me
We tried to repurpose Niggadom
To be a status of pride
Because we were strong enough to survive
But we don't thrive
So I'm tryna quit cold turkey
No Narcan can fix this maaan
No dolophine to help me ween
So, until I can get clean

And promote you
To the status you're destined to be
Imma hafta fire you from being my nigga
That position doesn't exist anymore

Danielle N Dixon
8/13/17

Stop Shaming These Sluts

Hypocrites know y'all need to stop slut shaming

Boy stop shaming these sluts

If you didn't need her then she would exist

Now you walking round like you wasn't tryna hit it

You acting like you wasn't the one all up in her dm

You acting like you weren't the one who askef for her digits

You acting like your hands didn't feel up her business

And then when she gave in you too good to be with her

Your fickle ass know you need to stop slut shaming

Boy stop shaming these sluts

If you didn't need her then she wouldn't exist

Now you walking round like you wasn't tryna hit it

You say she got daddy issues and can't treat a man right

You didn't have a daddy either and can't be a man right

You judge her cause she easy with the sexin and stroking

Like you the only one around here that allowed to be broken

Your pious ass know you need to stop slut shaming

Boy stop shaming these sluts

If you didn't need her then she wouldn't exist

Now you walking round like you wasn't tryna hit it

You say she's not wife material so you can be with her

So so deep fried and full of shit

Instead of tryna lay her down

What if you could build her up

Show her what a man's about

Show her that her true value's not in giving it up

Promote the ways that she's more than enough

And if you've ever had the benefit of getting serviced by a slut

Do yourself a favor son and keep your bigouth shut

You threw up the bat signal

And a slut flew in

Gave you pleasures that no other girl was tryna give

Ungrateful ass know you need to stop slut shaming

Boy stop shaming these sluts

If you didn't need her then she wouldn't exist

Now you walking round like you wasn't tryna get it

You say you want a good woman

But you're not a good man

Tyrna hold her up to standards

You don't hold for yourself

You know you went with the slut

Cause she giving it up

Passed up the good girl like she wanted too much

You can't change a ho to a housewife

She can't change a court jester to a king

You are the company that you keep

So

Danielle Dixon

You laid down with her she's your equal.

About the Author

Danielle Dixon is a poet and fiction writer from Cleveland Ohio. She got her Bachelor of Art from Kent State University. She has had her poetry published in the *Luna Negra* and *Inclusion Magazine*.

Danielle is an active alumna of the Cleveland School of the Arts where she assists with auditions each spring. Danielle has also been a feature NeoSoulPoet at Larchmere Arts and enjoys getting out to open mic events to test out new work.

At the time of the publication of this book, Danielle is working on a collaboration project entitled: *The Legacy Continues… A Muntu Poet Celebration of the Next Poetic Generation.*

This book is a companion book to Danielle's musical spoken word album entitled: *Sagittariusly BLUNT!* The book and album were simultaneously released in 2017.

Sagittariusly

BLUNT!

Danielle Dixon

UP**TOWN**
MEDIA JOINT VENTURES
PUBLISHING

Sankofa
Freedom Press

www.ingramcontent.com/pod-product-compliance
Lightning Source LLC
LaVergne TN
LVHW010027070426
835510LV00001B/13